I0484940

© Law Cheuk Yui / Michael Andrew Law. All Rights Reserved.

Copyright © 2015 by Law Cheuk Yui

All rights reserved.

Cover design by Law Cheuk Yui / cheukyui.com
Book design by Law Cheuk Yui

No part of this book may be reproduced in any form or by any electronic or mechanical means including information storage and retrieval systems, without permission in writing from the author. The only exception is by a reviewer, who may quote short excerpts in a review.

This book may include works of fiction. Names, characters, places, and incidents either are products of the author's imagination or are used fictitiously. Any resemblance to actual persons, living or dead, events, or locales is entirely coincidental.

Michael Andrew Law
Visit my website at www.michaelandrewlaw.com

First Printing: 2015
Shop Cheuk Yui

Michael Andrew Law
Artist Statement
「藝術家自述」

My paintings tries to captured the Soul of Youth , I combines classical mediums such as Pigment & Oil with contemporary painting method and medium such as Digital CG as Giclée Prints , I Only interested on ONE but immortal subject matters : Female Figures, by set against the figures with chinese calligraphy Employing the Idea of Word as Image, as an expressive scenario . I use both Life models and Computer Generated Images for the creation of works .

Through juxtaposition, both Icons (The Words and Female figures) , Both added meanings to the other.

These paintings are My Own interpret and to document HongKong's own Millennial and its Generation's view point and identities : As "Hongkonger".

oil on canvas 30x30"

oil on canvas 32x46"

oil on canvas 9x4'

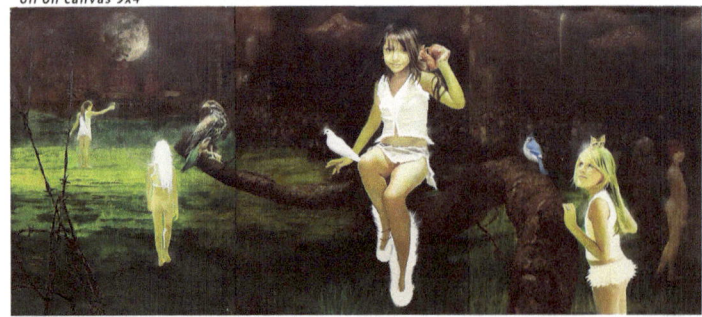

Painting by Michael Andrew Law
©2015 Law Cheuk Yui. All rights reserved

Michael Andrew Law at Work.

Michael Andrew Law

Michael Andrew Law (Born Law Cheuk Yui) was born 1982 in British Hong Kong. After studying Classical oil painting private lessons with New York Artist Daniel Anderson (1928 - 2008) at the his then-new workshop in Hong Kong, he made a stunning reputation as the designer of a number of cover spreads for the press in Hong Kong and abroad and as an illustrator and creative designer of various Comic Books / Story Books .

He then stepped away from commercial work and devoted himself solely to Oil painting. In recent years, he has aesthetically moved away from a stylistic "Icons Photorealist" to HongKonger-Realism, pushing his rendered subjects into a mythological arena. His artistic visions are treasured and collected by many . From there, Law quickly gained recognition in the art world by exhibiting at Hong Kong Convention and Exhibition Centre , The Avenue of Stars ; Law's works are also appreciated and collected by many Hong Kong and international collectors.

Some of Law's Religious artworks for Catholic Church of Hong Kong are also gained media attention in 2006 and 2007 ,and was also received by the Cardinal of the Catholic Church in the same year .

His Pale Hair Girls are a thoroughly subversive tribute to the world of appearances worshipers and to the Hong Kong's Millennial Generation culture of 21 century, with which the painter has cultivated an almost ritualistic relationship. His paintings provoke and compel. There is a unique realness in spirit.

The artist lives and works at Central District , Hong Kong.

Solo Show at NatureArt Gallery

At Ceremony with the Cardinal

Painting by Michael Andrew Law
©2015 Law Cheuk Yui. All rights reserved

Michael Andrew Law

(852) 6444-7550

info@michaelandrewlaw.com

www.michaelandrewlaw.com

HONORS AND AWARDS:

*Medici Cast Study Recognized by Social Fine Arts Grade Examination Center Of China Academy Of Art.
*Social Fine Arts Grade Examination Center Of China Academy Of Art Promotional Art(2011-present)
Publishers Weekly Best illustrated 's Coffe Book 2004 (Pete M.Parks)
The Salt and The Light Catholic Church Children Book 2004 (Mars)
Borders Magazine Most Original Voices nominee 2006 (Dear Fish)
Publisher's Weekly Best Children's Book list 2004 (America the Beautiful)
Communication Digital Artist -- Award of Excellence
European Print Weekly Design Annual Awards (2000,2002)
Face to face Dolphin art competition silver award 2006
Art Directors of HKC Award of Merit (2005)
Society of Fine Art -- An exhibitor 2005 Society of Newspaper Design Award of Excellence
Michael and Stephanie Duo Exhibition (2006)
Spectrum Fantastic Art Annual (multiple)
not-for-profit aution for Rotary of HK 2012

Art Funtion for
Organic Beauty opening

Exhibition :

2013 DeTour Matters 2013 Satellite Events at NatureArt Gallery
2013 December to Remember , One man show at NatureArt Gallery Central District, Hong Kong.
2012 Solo Show , Park Central tseung kwan O ,Hong Kong
2011 Art Walk Group Showing , Discovery Bay ,Hong Kong
2011 HK Gold Coast (Book signing exhibition)
2009 Solo Painting Exhibition The Avenue of Stars
Group Exhibition of Daniel Anderson workshop Classical Realism class of 2008 at Manhattan,NY
2007 Guest and ExhibitionThe Peak Galleria Hong Kong
2007 Invited workshop exhibition, Elements, Hong Kong
Group Exhibition of Classical Realism class of 2007 at Manhattan,NY
2006 Collection by Cardinal Zen Ze-kiun and exhibited at Catholic Church of Hong Kong.
2004 - 2007, Hong Kong Young Artist Group Exhibition, Hong Kong Central Library.
Group Exhibition of Classical Realism class of 2006 at East Village, Manhattan,NY
2005 illustration original exhibition for Kung Kao Po
2004 Group Exhibition, Wanchai Tower
2003 Group Exhibition, Hong Kong Convention and Exhibition Centre.
2003 Winner of I luv Hong Kong Painting Competition, exhibition at The Landmark (Hong Kong).
2002 The Holy story Picture Book illustrated picture original exhibition ,sai wan ho civic centre.

Art Funtion at
The Peninsula Hong Kong

SELECTED COLLECTIONS :

Cardinal of the Catholic Church Joseph Zen Ze-kiun
Organic Beauty Inc
Agriculture, Fisheries and Conservation Department
Ms.Ho Wei Ying
Ms. Annie Yu
Daniel Anderson
MR.Tsang Yan Sam

Interview with Hollywood Film
Producer / Teacher Dov Simens

PUBLICATIONS :

Fisheye magazine , featured artist interview , November 2002 (ISBN: N/A)
Kung Kao Po , interview , June 2006 (ISBN: N/A)
Art of Rock Realism , 2008 (ISBN: N/A)
Michael Andrew Law Early works Volume 1 - 3 :
(ISBN-13: 978-1503319400)
(ISBN-13: 978-1503366060)
(ISBN-13: 978-1503365087)
The The Pale Hair Girls of Michael Andrew Law , 2010 (ISBN-13: 9781503372115)
December to Remember One man Show Art Book , 2013 (ISBN-13: 9781505609257)
Christmas Everyday : Pale Hair Girls Christmas Series 1 (ISBN-13: 978-1505453218)
Christmas Everyday : Pale Hair Girls Christmas Series 2 (ISBN-13: 978-1505467796)
Christmas Everyday : Pale Hair Girls Christmas Series 3 (ISBN-13: 978-1505468052)
Christmas Everyday : Pale Hair Girls Christmas Series 4 (ISBN-13: 978-1505470741)
Christmas Everyday : Pale Hair Girls Christmas Series 5 (ISBN-13: 978-1505470857)
Christmas Everyday : Pale Hair Girls Christmas Series 6 (ISBN-13: 978-1505471151)
Christmas Everyday : Pale Hair Girls Christmas Series Specials (ISBN-13: 978-1505583922)
i-Egoism by Michael Andrew Law (ISBN:978-1-4990-2124-0)

Exhibition at
Hong Kong Central Library.

Group Exhibition at
Hong Kong Museum of Art

Exhibition at Avenue of Stars, Hong Kong (2010)

Exhibition at Hong Kong
Convention and Exhibition Centre.

Painting by Michael Andrew Law
©2015 Law Cheuk Yui. All rights reserved

關 於藝術家MICHAEL ANDREW LAW:

生長於交接時期香港的年輕藝術家 Michael Andrew Law，擅長把數碼繪圖，Pop 摩登藝術及古典油畫揉合時事及諷刺，創出獨特的視覺藝術語言及內容，跨越中西混合背景思維界限，探索互聯網世代交錯回歸的中西混雜之香港歷史。

他以自由隨意的手法結合摩登及古典材料與技巧，保持表現與認知、控制與隨性、魯妄與機智、自我與社羣等對立美學力量之間的張力，並對香港Y世代、本土文化及民族社會的殘酷現實作出尖刻的評論。Michael Andrew Law的作品色彩豐富，寫實風格描繪的冰山美人，刻畫在滿佈流行文化圖像、東方書法標誌及符號的背景上。《白髮女孩糸列》(The Pale Hair Girls，2006 — 2013 年) 的創作之中，Michael Andrew Law 獨特的繪畫風格呈獻出達達主義思考方式般的且出人意表的效果。畫中冰山美人式的人物穿插在抽象的香港和俗世符號上。

Pale Hair Girls系列的畫作的視覺靈感大量源自法國美術學院派大師William-Adolphe Bouguereau 的少年油畫作品以及已故華裔畫家陳逸飛的史詩及美人作品，Michael Andrew Law一反傳統的繪畫技法，以數碼混合古典繪畫技，重新演繹細緻複雜的中西方古典畫面和精心纖細描繪的構圖，以西式媒介呼應中國的傳統書法技作為圖案之筆觸，在Michael Andrew Law的筆下這種交錯西式POP ART和中式古典藝術表現時輪廓卻非常細緻，尤其最廣為流傳和臨摹的Leonardo da Vinci作品Mona Lisa (1517 年)，以東方血統之妻子肖像取代Mona Lisa 的表徵意義，極具質感的厚顏料同時呈現寫生畫作時人物肉體的細微變化。

《誰會理會不是自已的新天地:三聯畫》 (Humanity) 刻畫了在世代末日的未來世代們於本為廢墟的香港島上，等待著他們的命運。這些離奇的場景與Jerry B. Jenkins及Timothy LaHaye等當代作家描寫的超現實、宗教解讀、未來主義情懷如出一致。於半島酒店扶輪會演講當代藝術

主要探索他藝術裡其中一項最重要的二分法：浪漫與嘲諷、作為藝術家對美的浪漫思考與交滙中西混合背景思維之香港Y世代的悲情，由天真燦爛的冰山美人式少女與可怕的末日和俗世之間的強烈對比作象徵。無論是標誌性的單幅「古典書法圖案的無身份肖像」，抑或以三聯畫形式出現，運用到大師級繪畫與構圖技巧，揉合了精細傳統油畫技法與摩登畫的表現方式建構，美人亦在美術史和流行文化裡是永恆的主題。冰山美人式少女令人聯想到生命的脆弱與時光飛逝之無情。藝術家就是要了解不同世界之間的界線並翻譯到不同文化價值之間的語境如高尚對低俗、古代對現代、東方對西方。

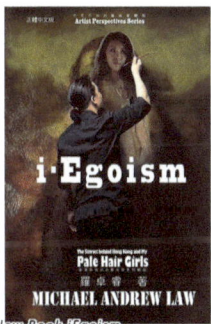

New Book iEgoism
ISBN:978-1-4990-2124-0

憑著 iEgoism 故事性的風格和精神，Michael Andrew Law將流行、古典與時事內容混合成一種感覺超豐富的視覺藝術作品，所涉獵的美學領域和文化靈感不斷延伸，而他在當中游走自如。一如常見的當代藝術主題，去作為「諷刺」及「反思」有關「浪漫」與「悲情」的直接敘述。

他所開發的iEgoism主題，就深受當代或反傳統藝術愛好者的喜愛，這被視為跟西方DADA藝術主義互相呼應。Michael Andrew Law把自己置身於他熱烈的自我網世代主義- iEgoism裡展現出的姿態卻是完全屬於他本人和他的時代的。

Michael Andrew Law於2006 年隨美國紐約藝術家Daniel Anderson深造古典油畫，其後發展純美術繪畫工作，2008年獲贊助於香港中環成立藝術工作室 Nature Art。除了製作藝術及相關作品，Nature Art 及 Michael Andrew Law 亦積極培育香港年輕藝術家。

2013 年，他於NatureArt Gallery舉行藝術展覽《iEgoism》，從香港歷史中追溯當代香港流行視覺藝術文化的特徵。

Michael Andrew Law 的作品曾於紐約 Chelsea 的聯合展覽中展出，他亦曾在著名機構及學校舉行個展及講座，例如星光大道 (2009 年)、天主教香港教區、香港中央圖書館(2004 -2007 年)、灣仔政府大樓外(2004 年)，香港會議展覽中心 (2003 年)。2015出版藝術文字著作《不可不知的藝術家觀點系列-iEgoism》更深入探討香港Y世代、香港歷史和Michael Andrew Law的作品脈絡關聯。

Michael Andrew Law 現於香港定居及從事創作。

Painting by Michael Andrew Law
©2015 Law Cheuk Yui. All rights reserved

Michael Andrew Law fusing digital and classical painting with west and East creative philosophy , to produce an extremely original artistic language and content that bridged west and east ,classical and modern medium , at the same time clearly tells the stories of his own generation. Combining digital creative materials and classical painting techniques with effusive yet knowing and precise focused , his paintings maintain a powerful tension between opposing aesthetic forces—expression and knowledge, control and spontaneity, savagery and wit, urbanity and primitivism—while providing satiric commentary on the oppressive realities of the predicament of Generation Internet, homegrown hongkonger's local-culture vesus Traditional Chinese culture, and The Hong Kong's post-handover history.

In his dynamically designed compositions, gracefully detailed figures and innocent faces are incise against fields that juxtaposed with portraits, chinese calligraphy, and sometimes cgi. The Pale Hair Girls Series (2006 - 2013) depicts realistic cold, icy-like young female figures surrounded by abstract and expressively painted forms and shapes revealing images of Pop culture, Historial figures, and Hong Kong landmarks.

Michael Andrew Law draws inspiration from Old Master's works such as Caravaggio , Ruben , Rembrandt , all the way to the Modern Art Superstars such as Warhol , Lichtenstein , Richter , De Kooning , Bacon , Wool and Prince . The Pale Hair Girls series mainly inspired by the painting works of French academic painter and traditionalist William-Adolphe Bouguereau and the Late Great YiFei Chen's characteristic "Romantic Realism" paintings.

In a reversal of standard East-West aesthetics, Law re-interprets Old Master's sophisticated imagery combine classical and digital materials—which resonate with Digital Vector Designs and Paintings—with fine strokes of oil paint multi-layered with paint film.In his interpretation of Leonardo Da Vinci's iconic Mona Lisa's smile (1517)—an iconic image that has been endlessly disseminated and reproduced—Law painted over the symbolism of the portrait Mona Lisa with his young wife , intent on rendering the figure in contemporary fashion with the iconic image as background .

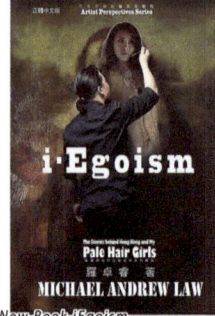

New Book 'IEgoism
ISBN:978-1-4990-2124-0

"The Humanity triptych" depicts New Generation HongKongers in a Ruined Hong Kong city , awaiting their unknown fate of a new beginning. This painting series explores one of the central paradox of his art—between romance and derision , his romantic magnanimity as an artist and his pessimistic perspective on the predicament of Generation Y Hongkongers. Here, this paradox is symbolized by the stark contrast of icy cold young female and disturbing representations of the armageddon-like of images. Whether portrayed as single "chinese calligraphy " or in triptych composition and classical paintwork that combine both expressive and traditional painting techniques with the digital vector , the beauties and the human figures stand as eternal motifs in the history of art and also in popular culture. Both oppositional and parallel, they are reminders of the fragile vibrancy of life and the impitoyable passing of time.

A references between different cultural refrence (high/pop, classical/contemporary, east/west), Michael Andrew Law has stated that an artist should be someone who understood how to hybrid between different worlds and go ahead makes an effort to knowing them. With his distinctive "iEgoism" philosophy , which employs highly refined academic painting techniques to depict a mixture of abstract expressionism within a representational pop culture images. These techniques parallel to the themes of romance and predicament of this generation , he recollects and revitalizes narratives of irony and introspection.

Michael Andrew Lawwas born in 1982 in British Hong Kong , studied fine art with american artist Daniel Anderson and graduate of China Central Academy of Fine Arts Sam Zeng from 2003 - 2006 . He co-founded the Hong Kong Art Studio Nature Art Workshop in 2008. In addition to the production and marketing of Michael Andrew Law's art and related work, Nature Art functions as a supportive environment for the fostering of emerging Hong Konger artists. Law is also a curator. In 2013, he organized an exhibition of contemporary art titled "iEgoism ," which served as a narration of contemporary HongKong Gen Y pop culture .

Painting by Michael Andrew Law
©2015 Law Cheuk Yui. All rights reserved

藝術家的觀點: 藝術天份

經常有人問的問題是做藝術作品是不是一定要靠點天賦 ？

首先要定義做甚麼藝術作品 ，若我指的是具像畫或雕塑 ，那種像文藝復興的畫/雕塑，所謂大眾基本上理解畫面是甚麼內容的敘事或描述式畫作確怎麼也要一點點時間練習的 ， 相對比較科學。畫那種天賦不是必要，卻必要有主動學習的能力和決心。

也即就 是要有學習的「天賦」， 也許和學別的任何東西其實沒有甚麼分別 ， 任何人要學任何一種藝術/技術也要有學習的主動能力和決心吧 ，那怕只是學用一個軟件，軟件造出來是為方便使用者吧，但至少也是須要使用者本身懂得怎樣用軟件去方便自己吧:

真實是有關製作技術的98%也是花在工夫和恆心上，關於這點沒怎麼大理論吧。

問題是若說做藝術作品不能單是靠製作技術的話，所謂的天賦便是指「創作的天賦」，要清楚說明「創作的天賦」在我的翻譯就是所謂的有想像力之餘，仍有能力去實踐自已願景的人，而不是單有想像力的人，想像力本身是沒有價值的，理由是，即是每一個人也有一點想像力吧 ，每一個人終其一生至少也會試過一次兩次有天馬行空的意念或夢幻想法吧 ，但也多數只停留在腦電波層面吧。

真正把這個腦電波寫下來，畫下來，計劃出來甚至製作出來，而再有能力組織，發表/公儲於世的又有多少人呢？ 多少人在起跑線上已經輸在覺得自已認為的「不可能」三個字而放棄了吧 ，也就是我所指「創作的天賦」，就是指那團覺得無論如何也要設法完成理想的火:這是大學不會亦教不了的 ； 也就是 Apple 在90年代末的Think Different 廣告所指的人 ， 在藝術界的邏輯上這些是偉大藝術家，在世界的邏輯上這些無論如何也要設法完成理想的人有的是大企業家，有的是大政治家。

但很顯然的分別就是那種幾乎是自我催眠狀態的實行力 ，而我說的實行力也不是指製作技術上；

例如，沒有甚麼秘密觸控熒幕不是Steve Jobs 發明的，手提電話不是Steve Jobs 發明的，在電話上使用的電腦軟件也不是 Steve Jobs 本人寫的，把三者綜合的技術也不是Steve Jobs 本人設定，就連把三者綜合的這個概念是否由Steve Jobs 首先提出也存有很多爭議；然而，iPhone ，iPad，iPod，iTunes 這些首先改變了世界規則東西也是歸功Steve Jobs，或是說 Steve Jobs 是整件事情裏最關鍵的推動器－而這就是我所說的實行能力。

這個就是我所指的「創作的天賦」，不是只存在字面上的天馬行空，而是實現天馬行空的決心，亦沒有藝術不藝術之分。

後話是，天份是否與生不俱來便「大鑊」了， 這個我說不上，又是一句「多少人在起跑線上已經輸在覺得自已認為的「不可能」三個字而放棄了」；然而，村上隆就在書中說了，「努力是必要條件」。

Michael Andrew Law

(852) 6444-7550
info@michaelandrewlaw.com
www.michaelandrewlaw.com

Selected publications

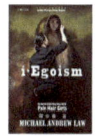

iEgoism by Michael Andrew Law
Softcover : 110 pages
Publisher : Xlibris LLC
ISBN: Softcover 978-1-4990-2124-0
ISBN: EBook 978-1-4990-2118-9

Michael Andrew Law The early years volume one: Nine Drawings from the early years collection
ISBN-10: 1503319407
ISBN-13: 978-1503319400

Michael Andrew Law The early years volume Two: Nine more Drawings from the early years collection (Volume 2)
ISBN-10: 1503365085
ISBN-13: 978-1503365087

Michael Andrew Law The early years volume Three: Nine Drawings from the early years collection (Volume 3)
ISBN-10: 1503366065
ISBN-13: 978-1503366060
Product Dimensions: 6 x 0.1 x 9 inches

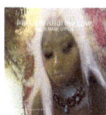

Michael Andrew Law: Pale Hair Girls Catalogue (Volume 1)
Paperback: 124 pages
ISBN-10: 1503372111
ISBN-13: 978-1503372115
Product Dimensions: 8.5 x 0.3 x 8.5 inches

December To Remember: Michael Andrew Law Exhibition
Paperback: 120 pages
ISBN-10: 1505609259
ISBN-13: 978-1505609257

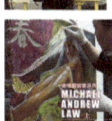

Hong Kong Artist Series: Michael Andrew Law 1
Paperback: 48 pages
ISBN-10: 1507580665
ISBN-13: 978-1507580660

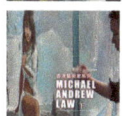

Hong Kong Artist Series: Michael Andrew Law 2'
Paperback: 48 pages
ISBN-10: 1507581556
ISBN-13: 978-1507581551

Painting by Michael Andrew Law
©2015 Law Cheuk Yui. All rights reserved

Michael Andrew Law

(852) 6444-7550
info@michaelandrewlaw.com
www.michaelandrewlaw.com

Publications : Illustrated Books

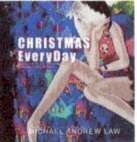
Christmas Everyday Book 1: Pale Hair Girls Christmas Series (Pale Hair Girls Christmas Everyday) (Volume 1)
ISBN-10: 1505453216
ISBN-13: 978-1505453218
Product Dimensions: 8.5 x 0.1 x 8.5 inches

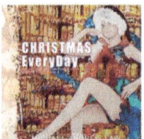
Christmas Everyday Book 2: Pale Hair Girls Christmas Series (Pale Hair Girls Christmas Everyday) (Volume 2)
ISBN-10: 1505467799
ISBN-13: 978-1505467796
Product Dimensions: 8.5 x 0.1 x 8.5 inches

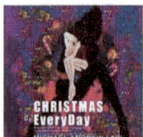
Christmas Everyday Book 3: Pale Hair Girls Christmas Series (Pale Hair Girls Christmas Everyday) (Volume 3)
ISBN-10: 1505468051
ISBN-13: 978-1505468052
Product Dimensions: 8.5 x 0.1 x 8.5 inches

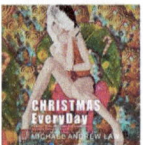
Christmas Everyday Book 4: Pale Hair Girls Christmas Series (Pale Hair Girls Christmas Everyday) (Volume 4)
ISBN-10: 1505470749
ISBN-13: 978-1505470741
Product Dimensions: 8.5 x 0.1 x 8.5 inches

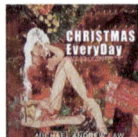
Christmas Everyday Book 5: Pale Hair Girls Christmas Series (Pale Hair Girls Christmas Everyday) (Volume 5)
ISBN-10: 1505470854
ISBN-13: 978-1505470857
Product Dimensions: 8.5 x 0.1 x 8.5 inches

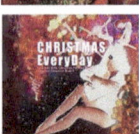
Christmas Everyday Book 6: Pale Hair Girls Christmas Series (Pale Hair Girls Christmas Everyday) (Volume 6)
ISBN-10: 150547115X
ISBN-13: 978-1505471151
Product Dimensions: 8.5 x 0.1 x 8.5 inches

Christmas Everyday: Special Edition (Pale Hair Girls Christmas Everyday) (Volume 7)
ISBN-10: 1505583926
ISBN-13: 978-1505583922
Product Dimensions: 8.5 x 0.3 x 8.5 inches

Painting by Michael Andrew Law
©2015 Law Cheuk Yui. All rights reserved

Michael Andrew Law

(852) 6444-7550
info@michaelandrewlaw.com
www.michaelandrewlaw.com

Selected Works for Art Events

iEgoism Exhibition at NatureArt ,Central District Hong Kong

iEgoism Exhibition In Photos (from left) : TV/ Movie stars Cherrie Kong ,Michael Andrew Law , Iva law ,Florence Lawman.

Michael Andrew Law exhibition at the Avenue of Stars, Hong Kong (星光大道).

Michael Andrew Law exhibition at the Avenue of Stars, Hong Kong (星光大道).

Art Related Events for Organic Beauty opening,

Art Talks at Credit Agricole CIB, Hong Kong Branch

Art Talks for The Rotary Club of Hong Kong At The Peninsula Hong Kong

Painting by Michael Andrew Law
©2015 Law Cheuk Yui. All rights reserved

Michael Andrew Law

(852) 6444-7550
info@michaelandrewlaw.com
www.michaelandrewlaw.com

Selected Works for Art Events

As Guest Art Tutor at Diocesan Boys' School

Working With Film Producer & Founder of Hollywood Film Institute Dov Simens.

Art Competition Award ceremony with Dr. Sarah Mary Liao , then-Secretary for the Environment of the Hong Kong Special Administrative Region .

Self Curated Exhibition with Art Collectors at Art Center ,2005.

Curated Art Events with The Swire Group (太古集團).

Curated Art Events with Hong Kong Stock Exchange (香港交易所).

Painting by Michael Andrew Law
©2015 Law Cheuk Yui. All rights reserved

Michael Andrew Law

(852) 6444-7550
info@michaelandrewlaw.com
www.michaelandrewlaw.com

Art Event with Young Men's Christian Association (YMCA).

Group Exhibition, Hong Kong Convention and Exhibition Centre.

iEgoism Exhibition

Exhibition, Elements, Hong Kong

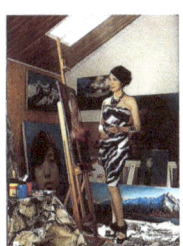

Oil Painting Shown in magazine :
壹周刊第1047期]第 20屆壹電視大獎 – 謝雪心

Painting by Michael Andrew Law
©2015 Law Cheuk Yui. All rights reserved

Michael Andrew Law

(852) 6444-7550
info@michaelandrewlaw.com
www.michaelandrewlaw.com

Selected Works for Art Events

Art Talk and Exhibition at Pui Shing Catholic Secondary School.

Art Talks and Charity Auction for The Rotary Club of Hong Kong At The Peninsula Hong Kong

Cardinal Zen Ze-kiun receives Michael Andrew Law at Ceremony. Comission portrait by Catholic Church of Hong Kong

Painting by Michael Andrew Law
©2015 Law Cheuk Yui. All rights reserved

Michael Andrew Law

(852) 6444-7550
info@michaelandrewlaw.com
www.michaelandrewlaw.com

The Pale Hair Universe Series

Medium : Traditional Oil Painting (With Acrylic Based) , Glitter , Gold Leaf .
About This Serie : Created Along with the First Series of painting of The Pale Hair Girls Original Series Paintings , Done with mixed media on canvas , with classical painting method.
Number of Paintings : 7 (As of 2015)
Availability : Limited Edition , Prints , Original Painting

Painting by Michael Andrew Law
©2015 Law Cheuk Yui. All rights reserved

Michael Andrew Law

(852) 6444-7550

info@michaelandrewlaw.com
www.michaelandrewlaw.com

Pale Hair Girls Original Series.

Medium : Traditional Oil Painting (With Acrylic Based) , Glitter , Gold Leaf .
About This Serie : First Series of painting of The entire Pale Hair Girls Universe ,
done with mixed media on canvas , with classical painting method.
Number of Paintings : 60 (As of 2015)
Availability : Limited Edition , Prints , Original Painting

Painting by Michael Andrew Law
©2015 Law Cheuk Yui. All rights reserved

Details

© Michael Andrew Law™ 2014.All rights reserved

info@michaelandrewlaw.com
www.michaelandrewlaw.com

© Michael Andrew Law™ 2014.All rights reserved

Painting by Michael Andrew Law
©2015 Law Cheuk Yui. All rights reserved

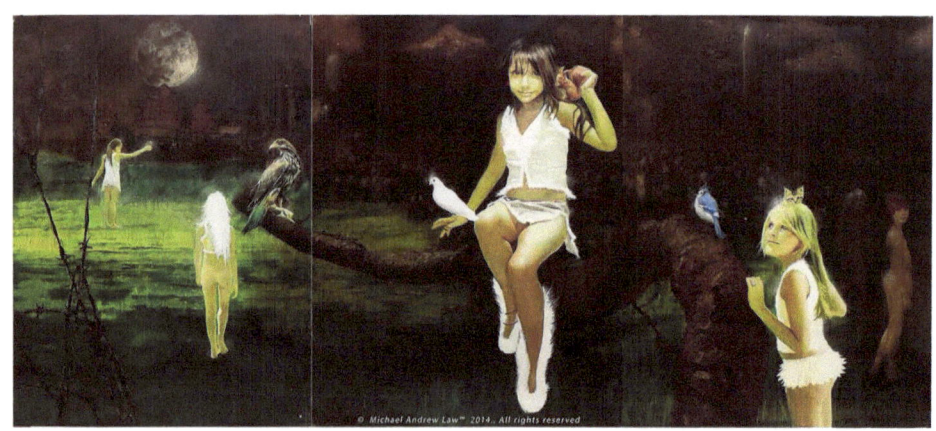

4'x 9' Multi-Panel Painting

info@michaelandrewlaw.com
www.michaelandrewlaw.com

© Michael Andrew Law™ 2014.All rights reserved

Painting by Michael Andrew Law
©2015 Law Cheuk Yui. All rights reserved

30x20 ˝ oil on canvas

S-P-R-I-N-G

info@michaelandrewlaw.com
www.michaelandrewlaw.com

© Michael Andrew Law™ 2014.All rights reserved

Painting by Michael Andrew Law
©2015 Law Cheuk Yui. All rights reserved

48x36 ″ oil on canvas

Nothing stops dreams

info@michaelandrewlaw.com
www.michaelandrewlaw.com

© *Michael Andrew Law™ 2014.All rights reserved*

 Painting by Michael Andrew Law
©2015 Law Cheuk Yui. All rights reserved

4'x 9' Multi-Panel Painting

info@michaelandrewlaw.com
www.michaelandrewlaw.com

© Michael Andrew Law™ 2014.All rights reserved

Painting by Michael Andrew Law
©2015 Law Cheuk Yui. All rights reserved

32x46 ´ oil on canvas

Somewhere beyond my reach

info@michaelandrewlaw.com
www.michaelandrewlaw.com

© *Michael Andrew Law™ 2014.All rights reserved*

Painting by Michael Andrew Law
©2015 Law Cheuk Yui. All rights reserved

36x48 ˝ oil on canvas

Goodbye Future II

info@michaelandrewlaw.com
www.michaelandrewlaw.com

© Michael Andrew Law™ 2014.All rights reserved

Painting by Michael Andrew Law
©2015 Law Cheuk Yui. All rights reserved

30x30 ˝ oil on canvas

I only dreams cause I am Alive.

info@michaelandrewlaw.com
www.michaelandrewlaw.com

● *Michael Andrew Law™ 2014.All rights reserved*

Painting by Michael Andrew Law
©2015 Law Cheuk Yui. All rights reserved

Michael Andrew Law

(852) 6444-7550
info@michaelandrewlaw.com
www.michaelandrewlaw.com

Pale Hair Girls : The New

Medium : Mixed Media Painting (oil and Acrylic) , Glitter , Gold Leaf .
About This Serie : Second Series of painting of The entire Pale Hair Girls Universe ,
done with mixed media on canvas , classical method crossover with contemporary Digital painting method.
Number of Paintings : 80 (As of 2015)
Availability : Limited Edition , Prints , Special Edition .

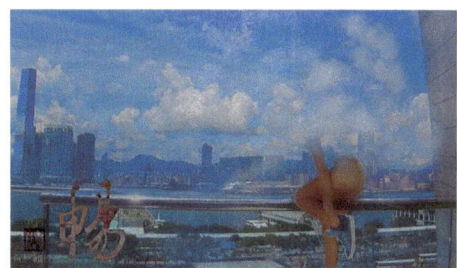

Painting by Michael Andrew Law
©2015 Law Cheuk Yui. All rights reserved

Michael Andrew Law

(852) 6444-7550
info@michaelandrewlaw.com
www.michaelandrewlaw.com

Pale Hair Girls : The New

Medium : Mixed Media Painting (oil and Acrylic) , Glitter , Gold Leaf .
About This Serie : Second Series of painting of The entire Pale Hair Girls Universe ,
done with mixed media on canvas , classical method crossover with contemporary Digital
painting method.
Number of Paintings : 80 (As of 2015)
Availability : Limited Edition , Prints , Special Edition .

  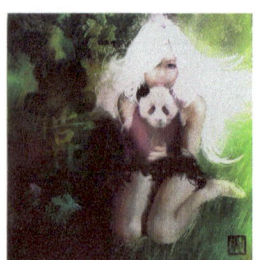

Painting by Michael Andrew Law
©2015 Law Cheuk Yui. All rights reserved

Painting by Michael Andrew Law
©2015 Law Cheuk Yui. All rights reserved

Painting by Michael Andrew Law
©2015 Law Cheuk Yui. All rights reserved

Painting by Michael Andrew Law
©2015 Law Cheuk Yui. All rights reserved

Painting by Michael Andrew Law
©2015 Law Cheuk Yui. All rights reserved

Michael Andrew Law

(852) 6444-7550

info@michaelandrewlaw.com
www.michaelandrewlaw.com

Pale Hair Girls : Christmas Everyday

Medium : Mixed Media Painting (digital print with Acrylic) , Glitter , Gold Leaf .
About This Serie : Special Series illustrations of The Pale Hair Girls Universe ,
done with mixed media on canvas , classical method crossover with contemporary Digital
painting method.
Number of Paintings : 102 (As of 2015)
Availability : Limited Edition , Prints , Special Edition .

Painting by Michael Andrew Law
©2015 Law Cheuk Yui. All rights reserved

Forgive the guilty.

Painting by Michael Andrew Law
©2015 Law Cheuk Yui. All rights reserved

am I allowed to go Christmas shopping?

Painting by Michael Andrew Law
©2015 Law Cheuk Yui. All rights reserved

Peace on earth will come to stay, when we live Christmas every day

Painting by Michael Andrew Law
©2015 Law Cheuk Yui. All rights reserved

How all of our hopes Had come down to this child

Painting by Michael Andrew Law
©2015 Law Cheuk Yui. All rights reserved

Michael Andrew Law

(852) 6444-7550
info@michaelandrewlaw.com
www.michaelandrewlaw.com

Pale Hair Girls : iEgoism

Medium : Mixed Media Painting (oil and Acrylic) , Glitter , Gold Leaf .
About This Serie : Third Series of painting of The entire Pale Hair Girls Universe ,
done with mixed media on canvas , classical method crossover with contemporary painting method.
Number of Paintings : 960 (As of 2015)
Availability : Limited Edition , Prints , Special Edition .

Painting by Michael Andrew Law
©2015 Law Cheuk Yui. All rights reserved

Michael Andrew Law

(852) 6444-7550
info@michaelandrewlaw.com
www.michaelandrewlaw.com

Pale Hair Girls : iEgoism

Medium : Mixed Media Painting (oil and Acrylic) , Glitter , Gold Leaf .
About This Serie : Third Series of painting of The entire Pale Hair Girls Universe ,
done with mixed media'on canvas , classical method crossover with contemporary painting method.
Number of Paintings : 960 (As of 2015)
Availability : Limited Edition , Prints , Special Edition .

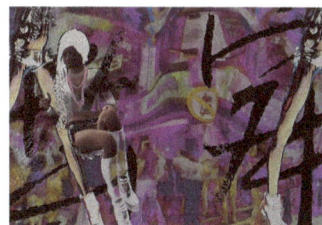

Painting by Michael Andrew Law
©2015 Law Cheuk Yui. All rights reserved

Painting by Michael Andrew Law
©2015 Law Cheuk Yui. All rights reserved

Painting by Michael Andrew Law
©2015 Law Cheuk Yui. All rights reserved

Humanity Triptych - Oil on canvas 4'x9'

Mr & Mrs .   Hong Kong Artist Couple

MICHAEL ANDREW LAW
八 十 後 香 港 藝 術 家 夫 婦

Most artists do not work as a couple, but many who do so succeed , such as Elaine & William De Kooning, Diego Rivera & Frida kahlo, Lee Krasner & Jackson Pollock, Franoise Gilot & Pablo Picasso, Georgia O'Keeffe & Alfred Stieglitz; artist couple are more than just working on artworks together, but its about the two artistic mind who have the deepest connection with each other , and take that power to make their biggest dreams ,come true.

Hong Kong homegrown artist **Michael Andrew Law** and **Florence Lawman** , both born into the 80s Pearl of the East Era of HongKong , growing up during the Pre and Post-handover decades, which was one of the most polarizing 30 years in Hong Kong history, with all the ups and downs in such a short period of time ; yet it also a time that needed Dreams more than ever ,**Michael** and **Florence** believe Art is the medium to makes dreams that can hold people together ,stay connected and happy.

Their works explore themes in a Generation Y perspective that characterizes the obsession with materialism and the vanity surrounding it . The archtectype is prevalent across Hong Kong pop culture since the 80s for what they grew up along with , from literature to movies , fashion , personal and social values .

Michael & Florence's works visually draws inspiration from Old Master's classical paintings by Caravaggio , Ruben , Rembrandt , tries to blend with Modern Art philosophy , inspired by Warhol , Murakami , Richter , De Kooning , Bacon , Wool and Prince . **f**   :   **L a w M a n A r t . c o m**
Website : MichaelAndrewLaw.com
Contact :(+852) 6444-7650 / 6743-1317

Michael Andrew Law and **Florence Lawman** work , live in Hong Kong with their daughter Hermione.

Article from Hong Kong Art Magazines Art Plus and Art Map
March 2015 issues

Painting by Michael Andrew Law
©2015 Law Cheuk Yui. All rights reserved

Michael Andrew Law at Work.

Michael Andrew Law fusing digital and classical painting with west and East creative philosophy , to produce an extremely original artistic language and content that bridged west and east ,classical and modern medium , at the same time clearly tells the stories of his own generation. Combining digital creative materials and classical painting techniques with effusive yet knowing and precise focused , his paintings maintain a powerful tension between opposing aesthetic forces—expression and knowledge, control and spontaneity, savagery and wit, urbanity and primitivism—while providing satiric commentary on the oppressive realities of the predicament of Generation Internet, homegrown hongkonger's local-culture vesus Traditional Chinese culture, and The Hong Kong's post-handover history.

In his dynamically designed compositions, gracefully detailed figures and innocent faces are incise against fields that juxtaposed with portraits, chinese calligraphy, and sometimes cgi. The Pale Hair Girls Series (2006 - 2013) depicts realistic cold, icy-like young female figures surrounded by abstract and expressively painted forms and shapes revealing images of Pop culture, Historial figures, and Hong Kong landmarks.

Michael Andrew Law draws inspiration from Old Master's works such as Caravaggio , Ruben , Rembrandt , all the way to the Modern Art Superstars such as Warhol , Lichtenstein , Richter , De Kooning , Bacon , Wool and Prince . The Pale Hair Girls series mainly inspired by the painting works of French academic painter and traditionalist William-Adolphe Bouguereau and the Late Great YiFei Chen's characteristic "Romantic Realism" paintings.

In a reversal of standard East-West aesthetics, Law re-interprets Old Master's sophisticated imagery combine classical and digital materials—which resonate with Digital Vector Designs and Paintings—with fine strokes of oil paint multi-layered with paint film.In his interpretation of Leonardo Da Vinci's iconic Mona Lisa's smile (1517)—an iconic image that has been endlessly disseminated and reproduced—Law painted over the symbolism of the portrait Mona Lisa with his young wife , intent on rendering the figure in contemporary fashion with the iconic image as background .

"The Humanity triptych" depicts New Generation HongKongers in a Ruined Hong Kong city , awaiting their unknown fate of a new beginning. This painting series explores one of the central paradox of his art—between romance and derision , his romantic magnanimity as an artist and his pessimistic perspective on the predicament of Generation Y Hongkongers. Here, this paradox is symbolized by the stark contrast of icy cold young female and disturbing representations of the armageddon-like of images. Whether portrayed as single "chinese calligraphy " or in triptych composition and classical paintwork that combine both expressive and traditional painting techniques with the digital vector , the beauties and the human figures stand as eternal motifs in the history of art and also in popular culture. Both oppositional and parallel, they are reminders of the fragile vibrancy of life and the impitoyable passing of time.

A references between different cultural refrence (high/pop, classical/contemporary, east/west), Michael Andrew Law has stated that an artist should be someone who understood how to hybrid between different worlds and go ahead makes an effort to knowing them. With his distinctive "iEgoism" philosophy , which employs highly refined academic painting techniques to depict a mixture of abstract expressionism within a representational pop culture images. These techniques parallel to the themes of romance and predicament of this generation , he recollects and revitalizes narratives of irony and introspection.

Michael Andrew Law was born in 1982 in British Hong Kong , studied fine art with american artist Daniel Anderson and with artist graduatee of China Central Academy of Fine Arts Sam Zeng from 2003 - 2006 . He co-founded the Hong Kong Art Studio Nature Art Workshop in 2008. In addition to the production and marketing of Michael Andrew Law's art and related work, Nature Art functions as a supportive environment for the

fostering of emerging Hong Konger artists. Law is also a curator. In 2013, he organized an exhibition of contemporary art titled "iEgoism," which served as a commentaries of contemporary HongKong Gen Y pop culture ;These Theroy also published in the book : "iEgoism" in 2014.

Michael Andrew Law currently works and lives in Hong Kong.

For further information please contact the studio at info@michaelandrewlaw.com or at +852.6444.7550. All images are subject to copyright. Artist/Studio/Gallery's approval must be granted prior to reproduction.

2010 Avenue of Stars, Hong Kong

Exhibition :

2013 DeTour Matters 2013 Satellite Events at NatureArt Gallery
2013 December to Remember , One man show at NatureArt Gallery Central District, Hong Kong.
2012 Solo Show , Park Central tseung kwan O ,Hong Kong
2011 Art Walk Group Showing , Discovery Bay ,Hong Kong
2011 HK Gold Coast (Book signing exhibition)
2009 Solo Painting Exhibition The Avenue of Stars
Group Exhibition of Daniel Anderson workshop Classical Realism class of 2008 at Manhattan,NY
2007 Guest and Exhibition The Peak Galleria Hong Kong
2007 Invited workshop exhibition, Elements, Hong Kong
Group Exhibition of Classical Realism class of 2007 at Manhattan,NY
2006 Collection by Cardinal Zen Ze-kiun and exhibited at Catholic Church of Hong Kong.
2004 - 2007, Hong Kong Young Artist Group Exhibition, Hong Kong Central Library.
Group Exhibition of Classical Realism class of 2006 at East Village, Manhattan,NY
2005 Illustration original exhibition for Kung Kao Po
2004 Group Exhibition, Wanchai Tower
2003 Group Exhibition, Hong Kong Convention and Exhibition Centre,
2003 Winner of I luv Hong Kong Painting Competition, exhibition at The Landmark (Hong Kong).
2002 The Holy story Picture Book illustrated picture original exhibition ,sai wan ho civic centre.

SELECTED COLLECTIONS :

Cardinal of the Catholic Church Joseph Zen Ze-kiun
Organic Beauty Inc
Agriculture, Fisheries and Conservation Department
Ms.Ho Wei Ying
Ms. Annie Yu
Daniel Anderson
MR.Tsang Yan Sam

PUBLICATIONS :

Fisheye magazine , featured artist interview , November 2002
Kung Kao Po , interview , June 2006
Art of Rock Realism , 2008
The Art of Michael Andrew Law , 2010
December to Remember One man Show Art Book , 2013
iEgoism , 2015

Solo Shows 2010 - 2013

I really appreciate your purchase of this Painting

Collection Book , I hope you enjoy reading them as

much as I enjoyed painting them!

May God bless your home with peace, joy and love.

From Michael Andrew Law.

Find Me Online.

Michael Andrew Law 🔍

www.ingramcontent.com/pod-product-compliance
Lightning Source LLC
Chambersburg PA
CBHW050827180526

45159CB00004B/1814